The Promise

a celebration of Christ's birth

MICHAEL CARD

A Sparrow Press Book
Nashville, TN

All songs written by Michael Card.
"Vicit Agnus Noster", "We Will Find Him", ©1991 Birdwing Music.
"The Promise", "Immanuel", ©1986 Birdwing Music/Mole End Music.
"Joseph's Song", ©1982 Whole Armor Publishing Co.

"Unto Us A Son Is Given", "What Her Heart Remembered", "Shepherds' Watch",
"Jacob's Star", "Thou The Promise" written by Michael Card and Scott Brasher,
©1991 Birdwing Music/Mole End Music.

All rights controlled and administered by The Sparrow Corporation.
All rights reserved. International copyright secured.

Library of Congress Cataloging-in-Publication Data
Card, Michael, 1957–
The promise: a celebration of Christ's birth/ Michael Card. p.   cm.
ISBN 0-917143-07-8: $9.95
1. Christmas--Prayer-books and devotions--English. I. Title.
BV45.C326 1991   242'.33--dc20
91-32862 CIP

THE PROMISE

HOW IN THE WORLD...

It's a steamy July morning. Though it's not yet ten o'clock, the thermometer outside is already pulsing past ninety. *How can anyone get themselves in the mood to write about Christmas,* I ask myself. How does one go about opening up the deep meanings of Christmas this day or any day?

At the heart of it, isn't that what needs to be done — to take off the wrapping that obscures the meaning of the Savior's birth, the way you might unwrap a long-awaited gift?

All at once the realization comes from beyond the world of this hot summer morning, shining like a star in a cold night sky, whispering like the voice of an angel, as simple and plain as a straw-filled manger: If Christmas does not mean everything in July, then in truth it means nothing in December. If I need a cooling in the weather and the sight of familiar decorations to cause my heart to leap like a lamb — if my heart cannot celebrate today as I consider the birth of our Lord Jesus, then Christmas reveals a problem in me. Maybe, 'til now, I've only been touched by the carols and tinsel, the *romance* of Christmas, not gripped with awe and wonder at the living Gift, delivered to us all on that first Christmas night.

The celebration of the birth of Jesus should be ever new. But for too many of us the scenery of Christmas has become too familiar and comfortable. It blocks our view into the depth of the stark mystery of it all. The mute plastic shepherds cannot speak of awe and worship. The posed porcelain wise men do not remind us of the search for truth. The tinsel star cannot possibly hope to kindle in us the Light that has come blazing into the world.

Perhaps the reason so many of us find it difficult to celebrate the birthday of Jesus is that we have confined the celebration, in many ways, to a single day — and, at that, a day that's become more cluttered than any other day of the year, a day that better represents the noise and business of all our other days. The task, it would seem, is to find afresh the meaning at the heart of Christmas. For when all the trimmings and wrappings are pulled away, the living heart of Christmas is a Child, a Man, a King, and we must discover, most of all, what He means.

What if Christmas day were both a beginning and an end? The

beginning of a celebration of Jesus that would not end until the next Christmas, when it would begin all over again?

What if the wisemen's worship and the shepherds' awe became, if not a daily then at least a weekly occurrence for us?

What if the peace and rest of the nativity became a part of every day?

What if Christmas were no longer a "holiday", but a *holy day*, infusing all our days with holiness?

These are the questions, the hopes I bring to the sights so familiar in my own mind — the star, the stable and all the assembled company of witnesses, in the skies and on the earth. I feel a deep need to ask of them: What is the meaning of this event? What promise lies here? As we begin, I confess I don't know what answers the Lord might give. I approach, armed only with the conviction that He *is* the Answer. And though He seems to give direct "answers" sparingly, He would not leave us without an answer to our important questions.

Where are you, Lord Jesus? Is seeing your face as simple as gazing down into a manger's hay? Is there a deserted stable somewhere, aglow with your Presence? Might I join a band of magi and follow a star to you? Might I keep watch with simple shepherds and hear the good news from Gabriel's own luminous lips?

Where are you, O Lord? Grant me the grace to find you again. Give me ears to hear angel words that whisper every day of you. Give me eyes to see the dim stable lit truth of your Incarnation every night.

Give me strength to follow, 364 days, whatever star might lead me to you on the 365th. That some day I might behold, unsquinting, the radiance of your Glory in a season that will be forever!

THE PROMISE

The Lord God said when time was full
He would shine His light in the darkness
He said a virgin would conceive (Isa.7:14)
And give birth to the Promise
For a thousand years the dreamers dreamt
And hoped to see His love
But the Promise showed their wildest dreams
Had simply not been wild enough

The Promise was love
And the Promise was life
The Promise meant light to the world
Living proof that Yahweh saves
For the name of the Promise was Jesus

The Faithful One saw time was full
And the ancient pledge was honored
So God the Son, the Incarnate One
His final Word, His own Son
Was born in Bethlehem but came into our
Hearts to live
What more could God have given, tell me —
What more did He have to give?

nd you shall call His name 'Jesus' because He shall save His people from their sins" (Mt. 2:21). Even His name is a promise: "The Lord saves."

Christmas is the celebration of the keeping of a promise. The promise that God would someday erase the sin of the world in a single day (Zech.3:9). The promise that He would someday walk with us, that we might be His people and He our God (Lev.26:12). The promise that the fall would be undone by the One who would crush the head of the serpent (Gen.3:15). A saving promise.

Faith, in the Old Testament, is defined by a person's willingness to wait for the promises of God to come. Faith, in the New Testament, means following the Promised One.

In that Promised One, God gave to us all He could give because a part of the "self" is given in the making of any real promise. Overwhelmed by His own desire to give, God sent the most treasured Gift to keep the promise He himself made. God chose to suffer the punishment which should have been inflicted on those who are guilty of breaking a promise. So for those who see Christianity merely as a relationship in which we can ask God for things, Christmas reminds us that He has already given His all, His own Son.

Christianity is founded on a promise. Faith involves waiting on a promise. Our hope is based on a promise. God promised He would be "with us", not as an unseen ethereal force, but in the form of a person with a name: Jesus. He promised us salvation in the name 'Jesus', by the name 'Jesus', through the name 'Jesus'.

> O Lord, how many are your promises? Are they not all "yes" in the name of the One who is the Promise? Father, let me spend my life pursuing that Promise. Teach me to hope in you, who always keep your Promise. Give my life to your Promise, so that I may shine like a single star in the darkness of this world with the light of your Promised One.

Unto Us A Son Is Given

Unto us a Son is given
Unto us a Child is born
He will be our King forever
He will reign on David's throne

Wondrous Counselor
Mighty God
Eternal Father
Prince of peace
Of His reign
And of His kingdom
Never-ending
Its increase

In love a throne will be established
In faithfulness will He sit down
For our garments, His salvation
Everlasting joy, our crown

He will be despised, rejected
A man of sorrows He will be
Cruelly pierced for our transgressions
Crushed for our iniquities

But His wounds are for our healing
And His punishment our peace
He'll bind up the brokenhearted
Grant the captives their release

Unto us a Son is given
Unto us a Child is born
He will be our King forever
He will reign on David's throne

n the waiting room of holy history, a voice, or a thousand thousand voices cry out, *"Unto us a child is born!"* To us and for us God has sent His Son. This birth announcement came not from angels but from the seared lips of the prophet Isaiah. And in order to fully grasp the meaning of Christmas we have to go back farther than the first century, we must go back to 700 B.C. and the ministry of this extraordinary man, a poetic old soul who understood better than any of the other prophets the full meaning of the word *Messiah.*

The clarity of Isaiah's vision is staggering: from the virgin birth (7:14), to the suffering of the Lamb of God (53:7), he saw that the "Holy One of Israel" would give Himself to His people as well as the Gentile world (42:6).

The birth announcement in Isaiah 9 opens with the great promise: "The people walking in darkness have seen a great light; on those living in the land of darkness a light has dawned." The "great light" is of course that selfsame Son who is born. It is the Messianic Dawn.

Then comes the majestic *catena* of "'throne names" for the Promised One, this royal Son of David:

> "And He will be called
> Wonderful Counselor,
> Mighty God,
> Eternal Father,
> Prince of Peace" (v. 6).

All we could ever imagine, could ever hope for, He is. He is the wise royal Counselor who fills us with wonder, who holds the tangled storylines of history and will one day bring true understanding between all individuals and nations. He is the God of Might, whose power can accomplish any and every task His holiness demands. His power we need not fear for He is also the Father Eternal who is tenderness itself and who is ever motivated by His everlasting love for His children. Finally, He is Prince of Peace whose first coming has already transformed society but whose second coming will forever establish justice and righteousness. All this, and infinitely more, alive in an impoverished baby in a barn.

That is what Christmas means — to find in a place where you would least expect to find anything you want, everything you could ever want.

O Lord, indeed you have given us a Son — your Son! You have kept the promise you made through your servant Isaiah. A promise you made to us. Lord God, we believe all the promises that are yet to be fulfilled through your Son. We long for the government of all the universe to rest, at last, upon His shoulders. We are weary, hungry for His everlasting peace to come in fullness. By your zeal, Father, and through your great love, accomplish all you have spoken.

WHAT HER HEART REMEMBERED

Out in the stable yard
She sees a glow
Could it be angel light?
How would she know?
Shepherds stand wondering
Afraid to come in
But the baby that's born tonight
Will free them all
To never fear again

As He lies in a cattle trough
She kneels by His side
Sweet baby breathing
Soft infant sighs
Soft sounds of swallowing
As soft fingers part
Marvelous memories
She pondered them and hid them
in her heart

Like a good
Mother would
She learned His cries
If He'd awake
With a bellyache
From hunger or fright
But now and then
Sometimes when
The dark would descend
He would weep
A dark so deep
For all her love
She couldn't comprehend

Her warm loving carpenter
His strong gentle hands
His dark and bewildered eyes
Can they understand?
That this Baby she's given him
Is theirs for a time
In truth came to give Himself
The Treasure and the Ransom
of mankind

he mystery of Mary, the mother of Jesus. It is she who submits herself, body and soul, totally to the will of the Almighty. It is she who simply "ponders" in her heart all the marvelous things God is doing in and around and through her. In giving birth to Jesus, she is the first to risk her life for His sake. She gives of herself quite literally to nourish the holy baby from her own body. All that the word "mother" can mean she was to Him, her little Jesus.

Mary was silent witness to His humble growing up years. From her open arms He set out to forever change the world. And to those same arms His bloody and broken body was returned after the world was done with Him.

I like to picture her years later. Now she lives in the home of the disciple John, to whom Jesus had entrusted her from the cross. Amidst the busy coming and goings of a household devoted to preaching and ministry, I see a gray-haired Mary quiet and calm, still the ponderer, wading through those marvelous moments that rushed past her like a torrent so many years before. She floats in the midst of them sometimes, barely troubling the waters....

The luminous angel. The great gift of Joseph, her tender husband now long dead. The night of Jesus' birth, the dreamlike quality of it.

All the infant tears she had wiped away. Holding His hands while He took His first wobbly steps. That awful fall from the ladder when He was a boy — the horror on His little face, the dreadful moment of silence before He broke into tears.

Then, much later, the evening He left home for the last time. The dark afternoon He died. The bright morning when He rose again. Seeing Him again, His countenance so otherworldly and yet still her Jesus. The same handsome face she'd caressed. The body she'd held close to warm with her own body. The perfect fingers she had kissed — the fingers of the baby, the fingers of the man...

As much as anyone could understand, that first Christmas, Mary was given to understand. The Life had come. A baby from a virgin's womb. A child that belonged less to her than to the whole world... But for a time, He was hers! He needed her. He couldn't have lived without her.

Luke, who gives us the nativity from Mary's point of view, records that once a woman shouted out from the crowd to Jesus, "Blessed is the mother who gave you birth and nursed you."

Jesus responded, "Blessed rather are those who hear the word of God and obey it" (Luke 11: 27, 28).

There is a good chance that Mary herself was Luke's source for that incident. And if she was, I believe Mary remembered it not because the woman had complimented her in a roundabout way, but because of her Son's response. She remembered, perhaps, how His words had stung a bit when she first heard them. But above all, remembered the moment when the truth of His words finally dawned on her. That those who hear and obey His words are truly more blessed than even she, Mary, the mother of the Son of God.

> *Lord Jesus, what does your mother mean to us? What can she mean to us? She was obedient. She pondered in her heart the mystery of who you are. Is she not a pattern for us all? What place should she have in our hearts? Use her life and her example to pattern our lives as you will, Lord.*
>
> *And if we are truly more blessed than she if we hear and obey your word, then, O Lord, give us ears to hear and strength to obey. And gift us with a heart like Mary's, to ponder the mystery of all you are!*

JOSEPH'S SONG

How could it be
This baby in my arms
Sleeping now so peacefully
The Son of God the angel said
How could it be?

Lord, I know he's not my own
Not of my flesh, not of my bone
Still Father let this baby be
The son of my love

Father show me where I fit into
This plan of yours
How can a man be father to the Son of God?
Lord, for all my life I've been a simple carpenter
How can I raise a king?
How can I raise a king?

He looks so small
His face and hands so fair
And when he cries the sun just seems to
disappear
But when he laughs
It shines again
How could it be?

J oseph is the mystery man of the nativity story, a missing part of the equation in the life of Jesus. In scripture we can gather basically three insights into his life:

First, Matthew is careful to tell us that Joseph made the decision not to publicly expose Mary — for what seemed to be a clear case of marital infidelity — before he was told the truth by the angel in the dream. Though he might have exacted the most severe punishment to either satisfy a bruised ego or even remain faithful in some sense to the Old Testament law, instead Joseph denies himself and in a sense takes Mary's "sin" upon himself. Later we are told that he voluntarily denied himself sexual union with Mary during her pregnancy, this despite no mandate against it in Old Testament law. In denying himself, in going beyond the letter of the law, and in taking upon himself what was thought to be the sin of another person, we see a man whose likeness was stamped upon a Son, though not the son of his flesh.

Second, Joseph is described in Matthew 13:55 as a *tektonos*, a Greek term that can mean "builder", "woodworker", or even "stonemason". Whichever is the case, he was a skilled worker, who possessed specific knowledge and tools for a job that was valued in his society. The scenes we might imagine, of Jesus in the carpentry shop being taught his trade by Joseph, are probably quite accurate. Jesus is described also as a *tekton* (Mk.

6:3). The fact that he was a craftsman points to a characteristic we see in other places in Joseph's life and that is the quality of patience, a quality seen in his stepson as well.

Finally, like the other great Joseph from the Old Testament, Joseph the husband of Mary was a dreamer. While she received direct angelic visitations from the awesome Gabriel, God chose to speak to Joseph through dreams, dreams to which he was always immediately and completely obedient.

Exactly what this says about Joseph is difficult to tell. What seems clear is that God knew he was the kind of man who could more easily believe a dream than a "real-life" confrontation. And if it tells us anything, it shows that Joseph was the right man for the task of foster fathering Jesus because wouldn't being the stepfather to God's Son be in itself a kind of dream? If Joseph whispered "How could it be?" when Jesus was born, it's likely he muttered it to himself for the rest of his life. For Joseph's life from that point on was caught up in a real-life dream, an unbelievable dream dreamt up by his Son who was, like his stepdad, a dreamer.

The full impact Joseph had on the life of Jesus would be difficult to underestimate. His common sense, his earthy wisdom, perhaps even his ability to tell a good story might have been passed onto his bright and loving stepson. From what little we can gather about Joseph it seems clear that his self denial, his manifest patience and his ability to see beyond the "real" world and dream of a world to come, were part of the legacy he left to his gentle, long-suffering, and mysterious stepson.

> *Lord Jesus, we thank you for your gentle stepfather, for all he meant to you and all he means to us. We understand that his obscurity no doubt pleases him, though it frustrates us, that he would desire our eyes to be on you.*
>
> *Even as you might have borne some likeness to him, allow us to bear your likeness in any way that we can. Let others see in us your patience, gentleness, meekness, lovingkindness. Speak to us in our dreams, whether they be sleeping or waking. Give us the strength to be obedient to your dream of the Kingdom that is, and is to come.*

JACOB'S STAR

A fire, a light
A shining star
A sign to those
Who'd journey far
A token from the King of Heaven
A spark as to the Light of the World

A beacon burning in the night
A star to echo endless light
A darkened world, a light from a stable
And high above the heavens ablaze

A star will rise from Jacob's house
A scepter out of Israel
And though thou art the least in Judah
O're thee oh Bethlehem
His light will shine

A light of hope to everyone
A light outshining every sun
A light the world has not comprehended
A light that is this holy babe

ne of the questions that haunts me most during Christmas is, why did God give the gift of His Son to me? Where does "worthiness" fit in? For, while I'd like to give myself the benefit of the doubt, by all accounts I'm not worthy. And neither are you. "God gives," Job realized, and though He sometimes takes as well, "blessed be He".

In the Old Testament God gave a glorious vision to a decidedly unglorious prophet named Balaam. The gift of the vision of Jacob's star to this betrayer of Jacob will always be a mystery.

Balak, king of Moab, was concerned by the large number of Israelites camped within his borders on the plains of Moab. They were amassing there for a planned attack on Canaan, beginning with the ancient city of Jericho. In reality the Israelites had no intention of attacking Moab. But still king Balak was afraid and sent his messengers to fetch Balaam, a famous diviner and prophet. After a couple of go arounds the messengers succeeded and God allowed the wayward prophet to return to the plains of Moab and the waiting king. (It was on this return trip that the famous scene with Balaam's donkey occurred.)

Balaam's fault was trying to play both ends towards the middle. On one hand there was Yahweh who he feared, whom Balaam knew was still in control of his utterances. On the other hand there was the wealth of Balak and the chance to cash in on his fear of the Israelites.

Three different times, in three different locations, Balak urged Balaam to curse the people of God. But quite beyond his power, when Balaam opened his mouth to curse instead beautiful blessings came rolling out. The effect on the king was not good to say the least.

Finally, when it was clear that curses were out of the question, Balaam proposed to Balak that he could still tell the king the future and what would be the outcome of his imagined confrontation with Israel. But as Balaam's fourth oracle came pouring out of the poor prophet's mouth the future looked less and less bright and after four strikes Balaam was most definitely out!

It was during that fourth oracle that Balaam saw far ahead into the future, farther even than he knew:

"I see him, but not now;
I behold him, but not near.
A star will come out of Jacob
a scepter out of Israel."

What Balaam saw was the Coming of the Messiah. It was this prophecy, uttered by Balaam, himself a wise man from the east, that started the magi on their journey to find the One about whom the star spoke.

It is not a very pretty story. It gets worse. After having failed to curse Israel Balaam advises Balak that the Israelites can best be defeated by allowing them to defeat themselves. In Numbers 25, we read of the outcome. Balaam was not able to evoke the God of Israel against his own children so he used the orgiastic Baal worship of the Midianites to seduce the Israelite men into fornication with women who were cult prostitutes. The end result of Balaam's advice is that 24,000 Israelites died. Jude, one of the brothers of Jesus, called it "Balaam's error" (Jd.11). His superficial faithfulness to God dissolved in the darkness of his treachery and Balaam later died in a retaliatory strike by the Israelites (Num. 31:7). In five books of the Old Testament and three of the New, Balaam is remembered as a scoundrel and traitor.

So the question is, why would God allow such a deceitful man a vision so glorious, a vision of the star of the Promised One. Wasn't there some faithful prophet around that God might have used instead?

The answer is that there is no answer and that those kinds of questions lead us nowhere anyway. God will use whomever He pleases, not always whoever pleases Him. He will bless scoundrels and liars with visions of stars and ladders that reach to heaven, while the "faithful" are left to pray and wait for such glimpses of His glory as they can find here on earth. He will embrace traitors and call them His friends because you see He is "for" the Balaam's of this world as much as He is for you and me — because in the end we're not all that different from Balaam with his divided heart and double-mindedness.

That too is part of what Christmas means. That we are pretty much all alike. And so we are, all of us, invited to come to the stable and stand together in the muck, looking to the One who has come and who promises to eventually lift us out of the muck. We are invited to worship One who was as ready to forgive and embrace an unrepentant Judas as He was a broken-hearted and ashamed Simon Peter. That is the Light that has come into the world, and it is only right that His birth should have been heralded by a star, a star seen rising a thousand years earlier by one who in the end is not all that different from you and me.

You are the Light of the World, O Lord. In you is no darkness at all. You are the light that enlightens every man and woman that comes into the world. Those who know you need never walk in darkness again.

But so many of my days are characterized by darkness, Jesus. And my nights are often darker than the night. Grant that I, too, might envision the rising of your star, that your Light might shine in me once more! Not for what I've done, but because of who you are, the One True Light.

WE WILL FIND HIM

On a day like any other
In our search to find the truth
We turned so many musty pages
In our hope to find some clue
Then the words leapt from the
parchment
From Jacob shines a star
That a wordless one who is the
word
Will be worth a journey far

We will find Him
We will find Him
We will follow His star
We will search and we will
follow
No matter how far
In castles, through kingdoms
We know where to start
To find the king whose kingdom
is the heart

It was a night like any other
So cold and black and dark
And it told us all too clearly
Of the night inside our hearts
Then the star tore through the
darkness
And like an angel shone
To guide us to that one true
Light
Who became flesh and bone

He stilled our secret syllables
And hushed our wisest words
In the silence of the stable there
Was Wisdom finally heard

We have found Him
We have found Him
We have seen the true Light
What was darkness
What was shadow
In His presence is delight
This One born so lowly the
heavens declare
Will someday reign without a
rival there

elchior sat brooding in his chamber, impatiently turning the yellowed parchment leaves of one of his obscure and valuable manuscripts. He was one of the chief magi of the Persian king. His reputation for wisdom and scholarship were well deserved, his grasp of the literature of all the world's religions was vast.

According to the laws of Persia, he had to be present at sacred functions to utter cryptic and sacred words known only to the elder and elite of his august group. Young "searchers" would come to him to seek out the deepest and most esoteric truths.

Melchior was a wise man. And yet...

As he slowly looked up, the parchment slipped from his long fingers and fell in a heap on the stone floor.

His servant, Aziel, spoke up, "Master, need I remind you to take care with the parchments?"

Melchior was silent.

Aziel collected the parchment leaves from the floor and returned them to their proper place on one of the long shelves that lined three walls of the room. Behind his heavy-lidded eyes Melchior was deep within himself, pacing up and down as it were. Searching. Wondering. The tormented habit of a lifetime. He was startled by a soft knocking on the door.

From outside, a youthful voice called, "Master Melchior, are you receiving visitors?"

"Come," he replied.

Into the room slipped a tall young man dressed in turban and the long-flowing robes of the son of a *vizier*.

"Would it be better if I came back tomorrow?" the young man asked respectfully.

"No, Caspar. Come in," Melchior replied, his impatience hidden beneath a tired, conciliatory tone. "What would you like to discuss today? Zoroastrian doctrine perhaps? Astrology?"

"There is but one question on my mind today, Master. Tell me — in your own heart, from your own experience — what is wisdom?"

Studying the old master's face, Caspar went on. "I have seen that wisdom is not the same as knowledge. I know simple men who are wise and knowledgable men who are fools. The one thing I do know about wisdom — the only thing I know — is that I desire it above all else. Beyond riches. Even beyond the love of a woman. And yet I don't really know what it is I desire, or why this desire consumes me the way it does."

Melchior was lost in reverie again. The young man's question had sent him on another journey inside himself. Caspar knew to wait in silence, for the old man was a long time in answering.

When he spoke again, Melchior's voice seemed weaker, "Your question comes as an *answer* to me, young one." He was whispering, as much to himself as to Caspar. "Your dilemma has given me a key to unlock my own prison. All my life I have sought wisdom. I have pondered the material world and the stars. I have observed mankind and sought to follow the twists and turns of his mind. Today, as I approach four-score, I realized that all my study has taught me that I know nothing. I have done nothing. Like you, all I am left with is the hunger."

Caspar was dazed. "Then what shall we do with our burden, this intolerable hunger for wisdom?"

"What can we do but wait?" Melchior responded. "We will pray to God — if a god exists, or if he listens or even cares."

Yet the tone of the old man's voice held little hope. And there was a heavy resignation in it which hinted to Caspar that they might never find their hearts' desire.

"Go, you have nothing more to learn from me," said Melchior sadly. "Come back if you find some answer. And I will come to you if I find one."

Caspar stepped out into the night. He looked up into a black sky, so much like the way he was feeling inside. *Not a single star out tonight*, he thought woefully.

The star first appeared, high in the western sky, four months later. It hung there next to Jupiter, the wandering star of the king, in a constellation the magi called, "the house of the Hebrews". Caspar ran, out of breath, straight to the house of Melchior.

Entering, he stared, dumbfounded. The furnishings, as well as the hundreds of manuscripts were gone. He wondered if Melchior had fallen out of favor with the king. There in the main study he found the magi at his window, gazing up into the early evening sky. His eyes were transfixed on the star.

"What does it mean, Master?" asked Caspar.

"It is Jacob's star," Melchior whispered. "The Jews have a prophecy, uttered by a disreputable member of our own society — Balaam was his name. It seems he was summoned by the king..."

"Yes, yes, I know the story," Caspar interrupted, barely able to control impatience. "But what does it...."

"*A star will rise out of Jacob; a scepter out of Israel.*" Melchior pronounced the words slowly.

"What does it *mean!*"

"It means that I have been an arrogant fool, young one. I have boasted all my life of being a seeker of truth — I, always me. When I saw that star I knew in an instant what it meant." Melchior sounded so forelorn that Caspar feared the star's meaning was something evil.

"That star is an invitation. You see, Wisdom is *seeking us.* And He has sent that star as an invitation to come to Him, yes Him."

Then the old man's entire frame shuddered, as a tear glided haltingly down his cheek and was lost in his beard. "All my life He has been seeking *me.* He is the one who has given to me and to you our hunger for Him. And now this star is a precious gift. I have sold all that I have for the journey and for gold to offer when I meet Him. I believe He must be a great King. Tonight I leave. I shall probably never return, never see you again, Caspar."

Behind the old man's words there was an awareness of his great age and the length of the journey. Evidently, he had accepted the fact that he would most likely die before he could return home again. At the same time his face shone with a peace that had never been there before, as if he had already found all that he had been looking for — his deepest longing already filled.

Caspar slipped up close behind him. He reached out and placed a hand on Melchior's boney shoulder, realizing that this was the first time they had ever touched. Together they stood before the open window gazing up intently at the star that was so bright it cast their shadows back onto the cool stone floor.

When it seemed that Melchior already knew what Caspar was going to say, the young man whispered, "Tonight *we* leave."

Lord, we would be seekers of you.
We would be the ones who embrace
your Wisdom. But it is you who
have sought and found us. It is your
Wisdom that has embraced us. It is
you who begin and finish it all. It is
only you.

"All who seek me find me," your
Word says. But are we not seekers
because we have already been found
first by you? And do we not find
you because it is you who have first
loved us?

Then seek us, O Lord, until we
are completely found. And draw us
close with your love, until we find
you forever.

VICIT AGNUS NOSTER

Vicit Agnus
Vicit Agnus
Noster eum sequamur

Did Abraham himself not say
God would provide a lamb
To take instead the punishment
That should belong to man

And so to humble shepherds
Was His glory first revealed
And with His birth a covenant
Made long ago was sealed

Vicit Agnus
Vicit Agnus
Noster eum sequamur

Out of His dark obscurity
The Light of God has shone
And through the meekness of the Lamb
God's strength would be made known

The just and gentle Promised One
Would triumph o're the fall
And conquer by His own defeat
And win by losing all

Vicit Agnus
Vicit Agnus
Noster eum sequamur

icit agnus noster eum sequamur is an ancient Latin motto. It means, "Our Lamb has conquered, Him let us follow."

Should the motto not read, "Vicit *leo*..." "our Lion has conquered"? What is the meaning of the words as they stand?

"Our Lamb has conquered."

How is it that we have come to follow One who is predominantly represented as a lamb? Where does the paradox come from, the one that teaches weakness is strength, defeat is victory, poverty is wealth? The paradox is rooted in this disturbing image of the conquering Lamb.

Throughout most of the Bible, He is not the lamb who conquers but the one who is himself conquered. In the Old Testament, the lamb is the helpless innocent substitute and sacrifice. It is slain to be consumed. Its blood is splattered on the doorposts to mark the homes of the faithful, so that the angel of death will pass over (Ex.12). The Old Testament lamb is victim, not victor.

Likewise, throughout most of the New Testament, when the Lamb of God appears He seems the most unlikely candidate to conquer. He is born in a stable, like a lamb. He is first recognized by shepherds who themselves have just come from the fields and the birthing of other lambs.

Except for a couple of incidents, primarily at the Temple when His "lionish" side surfaces, He remains the innocent, even weak lamb. And when

He is finally apprehended at Passover, He is slain precisely during the three-hour period when the other Passover lambs are being sacrificed, His own forsaken cries echoing together with the helpless bleating of those other sacrificial lambs. According to exact ritual observance the bones of the Lamb are not broken in the sacrificial process, not even by two Roman soldiers who, ironically, couldn't have cared less about ritual observance (Jn.19:31-36). And even as the other lambs are eaten, so He had earlier instructed His disciples to consume the bread that was His body.

Even at the moment of His resurrection, when we might expect to hear the roaring of the Lion of Judah, we instead hear nothing but the confused shouts of the women witnesses, whose testimony was unacceptable in their own society.

It is not until the close of the New Testament, in the book of Revelation, that the Conquering Lamb appears. Though still portrayed as a Lamb slain, He is yet the One who has conquered.

In the first scene, in Revelation 5, John is standing amongst a great crowd, witnessing an angel flying about with a scroll which no one is worthy to open. So caught up is John in the vision that he begins to weep. He understands that if the scroll is not opened history itself cannot unfold.

Then one of the elders, standing alongside John in the midst of the great crowd, says to him, "Do not weep! See, the Lion of the tribe of Judah... has triumphed!" *The Lion.*

So John looks up, blinking back the tears expecting to see a great, fierce creature. But what does he see?

"Then I saw a Lamb, looking as if it had been slain..." John sees, not a lion but a lamb — a triumphant Lamb, sitting on a throne! The unfolding image of the conquering Lamb has begun.

The second scene is from Revelation 17. John has been transported to the desert where he sees a woman, a prostitute, astride a detestable scarlet beast. A conflict is about to erupt between her dark forces and the Lamb:

> "They will make war against the Lamb, but the Lamb will overcome them because He is King of kings and Lord of lords — and with Him will be His called, chosen and faithful followers" (v. 14).

The final scene, in Revelation 19, takes place amidst the roaring sound of a great multitude in heaven. It is the long-awaited marriage supper of the Lamb, the final consummation of a romance that will last forever between the Lamb and His followers, His Bride. The context is exultant worship. The opening words are those of the thundering multitude: *"Hallelujah!"*

The conquering Lamb is finally wed. History has come to full blossom. It is the Kingdom. It is heaven....

Christmas, the celebration of the first Coming of the Lamb, looks back to the humble stable and the simple shepherds. The setting is a dark, fallen world. He has come to expose through His weakness the impotence of what the world calls power. He has come to show us that it is we who are upside-down.

In that sense, Christmas is a preparation for the celebration that will be the Second Coming, of the Lamb triumphant. The contrast between the settings of the two comings could not be more extreme. Instead of a silent stable and a bunch of motley shepherds, there will be a resplendent multitude whose praise can only be described as a "roar".

Oh Lamb of God, innocent, helpless One, born in a stable, held in shepherds' arms, sleeping in the hay. You are the Lamb, our Lamb, meek, gentle and spotless Victim.

Yet you are the Lamb victorious! You have conquered sin and death. You have overcome the evil one. The throne is yours. The glory yours. We look up to see the lion and yet it is still You that we see, both reigning and slain. And you bid us follow.

This Christmas, make us mindful of what your first coming means. Clear our vision so that we might look ahead and upward to your Second Coming, a faithful Bride, longing for the feast.

SHEPHERDS' WATCH

Shepherds watch, listening to lambs bleat
Tired backs, worn out and cold feet
All life long living like outcasts
All life long, longing for life

A dazzling light, the voice of an angel
Gripped with fear, terrified they fell
One like a man, yet awesome and holy
A face so fierce and yet strangely kind

"Do not be afraid, I've good news of great joy
Your Savior is come, He's Christ the Lord
As a sign to you the One born today
Will be wrapped in rags, asleep on the hay"

And all at once the air filled with angels
Glory shone, of holiness they smelled
"Glory be to God in the highest
And peace on earth to all those He loves"

he fire had burned low, as four exhausted men huddled around the embers. The spring air was pleasant though damp. They sat in the night poised, listening for the distress sounds of ewes who might be delivering their lambs. They were in the midst of the lambing season, the only time during the year when shepherds were required to keep a watch all night in the fields.

Already they had witnessed six lambs being born this night. Even for hardened shepherds, the sight could still bring a tear to the eye, though each would do his best to hide emotion from everyone else. This was not a job for sentimental men.

It was Nathan the younger who spoke after a long silence.

"Uncle, how many more weeks till we're done with lambing?"

"*We* might be done with it right now. The sheep, however, will probably be at it for another month," answered David sarcastically.

He was the chief shepherd of this lowly outcast bunch, yet he still commanded a measure of respect even among the other villagers. These men were on the bottom rung of Jewish society, barred even from testifying in a court of law. David knew the signs of the seasons and the sky. He understood the ways of the sheep better than anyone else in Bethlehem.

None of them noticed at first the light that had begun to glow behind them. It was, in fact, the smell of the angel that first caught their attention. There was a freshness about it, fresher even than the spring air that surrounded them, that awakened them with a jolt. Years later, any one of them would be vividly reminded of the angel whenever a cool spring breeze would blow across their faces. As they turned they saw the tall shining figure of a man, standing in the midst of the glow. But they knew this was no man.

Everyone looked to David to see what his response might be, whether to run or take up staff to protect the flock.

But David had fallen on his face. He understood who it was. The others followed his example and hugged the ground.

The voice of the angel was kindness itself, and filled with joy. It spoke with a laugh. His first words were those so often heard from the lips of angels, "Do not be afraid." The shepherds thought they could hear the hint of a smile when he spoke.

Then the angel paused, as if waiting for the frightened men to glance up and look him in the face.

"I have good news for you — good news of great joy!"

In the midst of what seemed a dream to the shepherds, they heard the angel speak a word that shocked them to full awareness. "Christ," he said, "The one born tonight in your city is Christ the Lord."

At this they tore their eyes from the holy light

that was the angel's face and looked into each others' faces. Each seemed bathed in a new light all its own. Wide-eyed they began muttering to themselves, "Christ, He has come! *Messiah!*"

As they looked back in askance, the angel seemed to understand that they wanted a sign, a way to find Him.

"He will be wrapped up in rags, asleep in a feeding trough," the angel said.

Puzzled, the shepherds had begun rising to their feet, moving toward the angel to ask more questions. All at once the sky exploded with light. It knocked them back on their faces. Squinting between their fingers they saw thousands of other angels, bathed in a blinding light. The sky was crackling and sizzling with the energy that surrounded them. Then a second explosion, this one of sound as the host erupted in praise:

"Glory to God in the highest,
and on earth peace
to men on whom His favor rests!"

Their eardrums all but burst at the sound of thousands upon thousands of voices. It seemed to the shepherds as if the host had been waiting too long to utter their praise, and now like a great dam bursting it came rushing out in one flood of sound, the simple men all but drowned by it, their eyes momentarily blinded, their ears deaf with ringing.

As they gathered their courage to take a second look the host was gone. Multi-colored spots danced before their faces. They sat blinking, sticking fingers in their ears, trying to wiggle the buzzing sound away.

Nathan's voice was hoarse as he whispered, "What shall we do?"

David replied, "What do you think? Let's go to Bethlehem and see this thing!"

They gathered up their cloaks from the moist earth and began sprinting towards the village. The youngest shepherd, still a boy, shouted out of breath, "What about the sheep?"

David's fierce glance back at him seemed to say, "The stupid sheep will be fine for now!"

As they entered the outskirts of Bethlehem, Nathan said out loud, yet still to himself, "Where in this shoddy village would the Messiah — blessed be He — be born? Even the finest house is a hovel."

"Didn't the angel say something about a trough?" David muttered, "He must be in a stable."

"I thought he said throne," the youngest said solemnly, "you will find him seated on a great throne."

"Your head was hidden under your cloak the whole time. How could you hear anything — you have fodder for brains!"

The next few hours the shepherds spent wandering from house to house, and stable to stable, bewildered and asking irritated people if they had seen a baby wrapped in rags and lying in a trough. It's not hard to imagine the kind of responses they got in the middle of the night from tired townspeople who had been wakened from a warm bed with such an absurd question.

The faint light of dawn was just beginning to glow in the eastern sky.

"There's no baby," one of them grumbled. "We've been duped, don't ask me how. We're going back to check on the flock."

As two of the shepherds trudged off towards the fields, Nathan and David looked bewildered at each other. There was a sort of tired panic on their faces.

"How could they?" Nathan gasped in amazement.

"Perhaps there's some hidden meaning," David spoke, exhausted. "Maybe it's not as simple as we thought. We'll ask the rabbi in the morning, if anyone in town is still speaking to us."

They stood in the middle of a small square, tired and confused, about to follow their friends when they thought they heard the faintest sound of the crying of a newborn baby. It sounded to them almost like the bleating of a newborn lamb....

*We thank you Lord for coming to
and for all of us. For the foolish and
the wise, the rich and the poor.*

*That you would send angels to
outcast shepherds to tell even them of
the good news. That you would
allow men who were disqualified in
their day as witnesses to nonetheless
witness your Coming. You are no
respecter of persons, yet you are the
great respecter of us all. Caring to
communicate to all, to reach out to
all, to die for all, even those who
would not return your love.*

*We praise you, O Lord, for
entrusting us with your good news!*

THOU THE PROMISE

Thou the Promise
And Keeper of the promise
Our Salvation
And our only Savior
Our redemption
Our Redeemer
Thou art ours
And we are Thine

Savior, Servant
Deliverer, Messiah
Our great King, Desire of all Nations
Tired eyes at last can see you
Longing lips can speak your name

Jesus Christ
Jesus Christ
Jesus Christ

Thou the Lamb
And yet the Shepherd
Thou the Lamb
And yet the Lion
Thou great Judge
And selfsame Savior
In wonder we cry out to thee

I f faith, for us, does mean *following*, then I believe it will one day carry us to a point when we begin to glimpse all that Christ means. And in that moment, the rush of joy and celebration may resemble the frenzy you see on the face of someone who, in the midst of opening a Christmas gift, realizes that it is the one present they have been hoping for. A sort of holy panic.

You can hear the tone of it in Colossians 1 as Paul gets caught up in the sheer weight of the glory of it:

> He is the image of the invisible God, the firstborn of all creation. For by Him all things were created: things in heaven and on earth, visible and invisible, whether thrones or powers or rulers or authorities; all things were created by Him and for Him
> (vv. 15, 16).

He seems exhausted and out of breath by verse 20:

> ...through [Jesus Christ, God] was pleased to reconcile to himself all things, whether things on earth or things in heaven, by making peace through His blood, shed on the cross.

John says the whole world could not contain the books that could be written about Him (Jn.21:25).

It is this almost hopeless feeling of inadequacy to communicate His awesomeness that gives passion to our worship.

If this Christmas does nothing more than pass on to us this frustrating, holy panic, it has not been in vain.

Lord Jesus, you fill everything in every way. The whole universe is filled with your glory. You fill our hearts with praise, love and longing for you. You fill our minds with wonder. You fill our souls with hope. You fill our mouths with words that make us stammer and stutter before the world in trying to tell all that you mean, all that you are.

You are Lamb and Lion. The Light that has come radiant, shining into the world. The Truth. The Way. You are Immanuel: "God with us." The First and the Last, the Alpha and Omega. The Son of God, and Son of Man.

There are not enough words to say all that you are. We have not enough breath to speak it. But now in the sacrament of this present moment, hear us Jesus as we confess, YOU ARE LORD!

IMMANUEL

A sign shall be given
A virgin will conceive (Isa.7:14)
A human baby bearing
Undiminished Deity
The glory of the nations
(Ps.96:3,39:21)
A light for all to see
And hope for all who will
embrace
His warm reality

Immanuel
Our God is with us (Mt.1:23)
And if God is with us
Who could stand against us
(Rom.8:31)
Our God is with us
Immanuel

For all those who live in the
shadow of death
A glorious light has dawned
(Isa.9:2)
For all those who stumble in the
darkness
Behold your light has come!
(Isa.60:1)

Immanuel
Our God is with us
And if God is with us
Who could stand against us
Our God is with us
Immanuel

So what will be your answer?
Oh will you hear the call?
Of Him who did not spare His
son
But gave him for us all
On earth there is no power
There is no depth or height
That could ever separate us from
the love (Rom.8:35)
of God in Christ

Immanuel
Our God is with us
And if God is with us
Who could stand against us
Our God is with us
Immanuel

n the darkness of the night,
He is with us!
In our stable-like poverty,
He is with us!
As we face up to death,
He is with us!
In our deepest longing to embrace true life,
He is with us!

His name is Immanuel, "our God is with us."

The name is a promise, as He is the Promise. It describes what He means, or what He can mean. It is the name that contains our hope, and His. He is with us, He is for us. He is Immanuel. He is our God. Long before His first Coming it was nonetheless still His name.

Lord Jesus, you kept your
Promise. You came to us. You
departed; yet you stayed. You were
present, and are present still to the
senses of faith. You are Immanuel,
our God who is with us. Having
you, our only fear would be to have
you no longer. But you have
promised never to leave. Thank you
for that promise, Jesus.

Lord, forgive us for we hunger to
see your face with our eyes, to hear
your voice with human ears, to feel
your hand in ours. Are we hungry
because our faith is weak and too
feeble to see you in the present? Or
is our hunger for you because of
faith, is it your gift to us? Is our
longing to see you a part of seeing
you? Do we seek you because we
have already been found by you?

Speak, touch, appear — come,
Lord Jesus! Make yourself fully
known as Immanuel to us!

Conclusion

At the beginning of our journey together, I confessed not knowing what the final answer to the "problem" of Christmas might be. While I still cannot claim a definitive solution, I feel a bit closer to it.

The problems of Christmas — the over-connectedness to the season and the obscurity caused by our over-familiarity with it — are not insurmountable. To find our way we must always go back to the essence of meaning of the various stories of Christmas. And in this way, we will continue to discover the ever-new lessons of Christmas, lessons which belong to the entire year, to every moment of every day.

These are a few lessons I have gathered along the way:

The lesson of the Incarnation. The lesson here is that there is no "lesson": The Incarnation is not simply a mystery, it is *the* mystery. The mystery of it calls forth *worship.*

The lesson of Paradox. At Christmas we see the King of the Universe wrapped in rags, asleep in a feeding trough, God becoming man. It is not that these paradoxes are ultimately irrational, as some accuse them of being, they are *super-rational.* They come from a God who is infinitely bigger than we are. They cannot be deciphered in this life since they cannot be fully grasped by the mind. Therefore they call forth faith.

The lesson of the wise men. We saw that magi, traditionally viewed as seekers of truth, were in truth the ones who were sought, who were invited by the star of Jacob to come and look Wisdom in the face. This exposing of their pride and ours calls forth *humility.*

The lesson of the shepherds. Finally, as we witnessed God's reaching out to the shepherds, the outcasts of their day, we saw that He is a God who reaches out to us all. No matter how sinful or lowly. This calls forth *thanksgiving.*

By no means is my list exhaustive. It represents only the beginning of that process of unwrapping the gift of what He means. It is up to you to seek and unwrap the Promise for yourself.

We saw that it all began with a promise. It came to fulfillment when the Promise became a person in Christ Jesus. And to this moment it is all sustained by the powerful Word of His Promise.

He promised to come to us. And He did.
He promised to save us. And He has.
He promised to come again. And He will.
He is the Promise.
He is God's great gift.

> *Lord Jesus, let this Christmas be a time*
> *of looking back more clearly than we ever*
> *have at all your first coming means.*
> *Transform our lives by it. Make us lights*
> *in this dark world during a season that for*
> *many is the darkest time of the year.*
> *Comfort us with your real presence. Give us*
> *hearts to ponder the depth of the mystery of*
> *you. Help us to see the precious place you*
> *have for each of us in your plan.*
>
> *Thank you Lord, for seeking us first —*
> *for loving us first and thereby enabling us*
> *to seek and love you. Thank you for giving*
> *your life that we might live in your*
> *presence in a season that will be forever.*
>
> *Thank you for coming. Even so, Come,*
> *Lord Jesus!*